French Cookin_ the Lewis R. French

By Kathy Pease and Kathleen Ganster
Pittsburgh, PA
2003

Cover design and illustrations by Patricia A. Menick

For additional copies, use the order forms in the back of the book or write directly to:

Traveling Bag Press
P.O. Box 273
Allison Park, P A 15101-0273
724-443-1664 or email kganster@fyi.net
Or

Schooner Lewis R. French
P.O. Box 922
Camden, ME 04843
1-800-469-4635 or email windjam@midcoast.com

ISBN 0-9728736-0-0

Dedication

To my husband, Captain Dan, and our sons, Joe and Billy, for whom I love to cook. - KP

To my mother, Lillian Ganster, who always thought I should be a writer and according to my children, is the best cook in the world. And to my dad, William Ganster, for always being my hero.
- KJG

Table of contents

Introduction

Why a cookbook from a tallship cruise?
There is no doubting the natural beauty of the state of Maine.
And what better way to experience that beauty than in a tall
ship, sailing up the coast? When we decided to take a sail on
the Lewis R. French, one of the ships in the Maine
Windjammer Fleet, I had hoped for a relaxing trip and as a
travel and food writer, a couple of good stories. Well, I did get
my stories, but I also experienced some of the best food that I
had ever eaten!

Waking up in the morning, smelling the fresh baked muffins
and coffee...fresh breads and delicious breakfast foods
(including Lewis R. French toast)...more fresh breads with
soups and salads...yummy snacks...and finally, wonderful
dinners. The food was outstanding. One of the return
passengers said that on every trip he took, many folks would sit
in the galley, copying the recipes. No wonder. It seems the
Lewis R. French was well known not only for the sailing
adventures but also for the meals served on the cruises.

While researching my stories, I learned the recipes came from
Kathy Pease, co-owner of the French with her husband,
Captain Dan. The recipes were in a blue binder marked "Bible"
– appropriate indeed for the fine foods we were served. I too
copied several recipes. The recipes are a cumulation over the
years – Kathy created many of these recipes; some came from
other cooks of the Lewis R. French, and Kathy recreated others
after many hours of pouring through cookbooks.

Later while chatting with Kathy for one of my articles, she said, "Someday I want to write a cookbook." I thought, "Why not now?" When I suggested the idea to her that we co-write it, she was as excited about it as I. I set about testing Kathy's recipes and downsizing them.

Boat cooking has its own unique set of challenges and issues. One of the issues with boat cooking is that you have to make enough for a whole boatload – 22 passengers and four hungry crew members. Most home cooks don't need to feed that many in one sitting!

Another issue is that the chefs do all their cooking on and in a woodburning stove in the rather small galley. Talk about challenges. Fortunately, most of us have modern ovens in our own home kitchens so we adapted the recipes for that as well.

Some of the ingredients may be hard to find in certain parts of the country. Feel free to make appropriate substitutions and have fun with these recipes. After all, that is what the Windjammer cruises are all about – having great fun.

Both Kathy and I have comments throughout the book. Kathy's initials will follow her comments (KP) and mine will follow my comments (KJG). Happy cooking and happy sailing in your adventures in life.

---Kathleen Ganster

About the Lewis R. French

The Lewis R. French is the oldest schooner in the Maine Windjammer fleet. She was honored by the National Historic Register and is a National Historic Landmark. She was launched into Christmas Cove, Maine on April 28, 1871. Even though she is over 125 years old, the French has continuously worked for her living, freighting cargoes including lumber, firewood, bricks, granite, fish, lime, people and Christmas trees.

After her third major rebuild (1900, 1930, and 1976), being renewed from keel to topmasts, the French was brought into passenger service in 1976.

The French is 101 feet overall, 65 feet on deck, 19 feet beam, and draws 7.5 feet of water with a full keel. She is made out of native red oak and white pine. There is no inboard engine, so there are a lot of sails – about 3,000 square feel work, including the two topsails. The French can carry 22 passengers in both single and double rooms. The galley can seat 25 and is often a meeting room for a quick game of cards or quiet place to read.

The French is also a great sailor and has won the Coaster Class of the Great Schooner Race several times. She also sailed to Boston to participate in the SAIL BOSTON tall ships regatta in 1992 and 2000.

Captain Dan and Kathy Pease have owned the French since 1986. Dan was born in Maine and has lived his whole life along the coast of Maine! He leaned to sail from his father and his love of sailing took him to the U.S. Coast Guard Academy where he studied civil engineering. He has built, rebuilt, and sailed more than a few boats on his way to owning and skippering the Lewis R. French. During the off-season, he likes to build wooden boats at home in his boatshop.

Kathy was born and raised in Wisconsin, and first came to Maine to go windjamming in 1981. It was an experience she never forgot and hoped to duplicate in 1988 when she came back and sailed on the Lewis R. French. There she met Capt. Dan, and soon was working as the cook on the schooner. The two married and together they run every aspect of the Lewis R. French, with Kathy overseeing the office and the galley. She's usually at home with their two sons, where she does the office work. Kathy also keeps busy cooking up jams and pickles plus granola for the schooner. Sometimes she still gets on board to cook for the passengers.

Their two sons, Joe and Bill, who sometimes sail as crew on the French, round out the Pease family. The family lives in Rockport with their four cats.

The French is harbored in Camden, a small, storybook village typical of many Maine seaports. The town is known as "where the mountains meet the sea." The village has many shops and restaurants.

Muffins, muffins and more muffins...

On the Windjammer cruise, there is nothing like the smell of freshly brewed coffee and warm muffins on a chilly morning. The muffins that are served fresh out of the oven every morning on the boat at 7 a.m. promise to lure even the sleepiest of passengers out of their cabins. These muffins will also please your own crew at home.

Before you begin, some muffin baking tips:
- Always measure all of your dry ingredients into a separate bowl and mix together before mixing in wet ingredients. This is very important.
- You will also mix all of the wet ingredients together in a separate bowl before adding to the dry ingredients. These two steps guarantee ingredients will be properly mixed.
- When adding the wet ingredients to the dry ingredients, you will stir only until blended. Don't beat your muffin mixture! If you overmix, you will have tough muffins.
- Spray your muffin tins with a non-stick spray. Spray in between the muffin cups so that any over-spill also easily lifts off.
- Fill the muffin tins about 2/3 of the way full to leave room for rising during baking.
- All of these muffins freeze very well. Pop some in a freezer bag and kids can take them out one at a time then thaw them in the microwave for a quick breakfast or snack. They also can be added to a school lunch in the morning and will be thawed by lunchtime.
- You can also make these in miniature muffin tins. My kids love these mini-muffins.

- Kathy and the chefs on the Lewis R. French always use unbleached King Arthur Flour. Happily, this fine New England product is now available in stores across the United States or by mail order (see resource list). When called for, we also used King Arthur Whole Wheat Flour.
- Always preheat the oven before baking.

Apple Muffins

½ cup butter, soft
½ cup packed brown sugar
¾ cup sugar
2 eggs
1 ¼ cup apple cider (can use buttermilk instead)
4 cups flour
3-tablespoons cinnamon
1-tablespoon baking soda
½ teaspoon salt
2 cups Macintosh apples, peeled and diced*
extra brown sugar

Preheat oven to 400 degrees. Mix together butter, brown sugar, sugar, eggs and apple cider in a bowl. Combine flour, cinnamon, baking soda and salt in a separate, larger bowl. Add smaller bowl to larger bowl, mixing until lumps are gone but don't over mix. Fold in apple pieces. Spoon into greased muffin tins, sprinkle lightly with brown sugar. Bake at 400 degrees for about 20 minutes.

*You can cut up the apples the day before to save time in the morning.

Makes about 2 dozen muffins.

Banana Rum Muffins

Why didn't the chef make these muffins when we were on the cruise? These muffins are incredibly moist and delicious. Don't be worried about the rum if you have children. The rum taste isn't overwhelming at all and my own three loved them. KJG

3 cups flour
2 cups sugar
2 teaspoons salt
2 teaspoons baking soda
1-teaspoon nutmeg
¼ teaspoon ground ginger*
¾ cup oil
2 eggs
6 mashed bananas
¼ cup rum (can use orange juice instead if you don't like the rum)

Preheat the oven to 400 degrees. Prepare the muffin tins.
Mix the flour, sugar, salt, baking soda and nutmeg in a large bowl. If you are using ginger and nutmeg, add those as well.
In a separate bowl, mix the oil, eggs, bananas and rum.
Pour the oil and egg mixture into the flour mixture. Stir until just combined. Spoon into prepared muffin tins. The mixture will be a little sticky because of the rum. Bake at 400 degrees for approximately 20 minutes or until inserted toothpick comes out clean.

*Optional. Add the ginger for more of a Caribbean flavor.

Makes about two dozen generous sized muffins.

Banana Streusel Muffins

Muffin:
3 cups flour
4-teaspoons baking powder
½ teaspoon baking soda
pinch salt
2-tablespoons ground ginger
½ teaspoon nutmeg
1-cup brown sugar
4 eggs
2 cups sour cream
2-tablespoons butter, melted
6 ripe bananas

Preheat oven to 400 degrees. Combine flour, baking powder, baking soda, salt, ginger, and nutmeg in a large bowl. In a separate, smaller bowl mix brown sugar, eggs, sour cream, and the melted butter. Stir in bananas. Add to dry ingredients mixing just until combined. Top with streusel topping.

Streusel Topping:
½ cup flour
½ cup shredded coconut
¼ cup plus 2 tablespoons brown sugar
½ teaspoon nutmeg
4 tablespoons melted butter

Combine all ingredients except the butter. Add melted butter; stir until mixture is moist and crumbly. Put on top of muffins. Bake at 400 degrees for approximately 20 minutes.

Blueberry Corn Muffins

The combination of blueberries with the corn meal is delicious. There are nice at dinner as well as for breakfast. KJG

3 cups flour
1-cup corn meal
1 tablespoon plus 2 teaspoons baking powder
1 ½ teaspoons salt
½ cup sugar
3 eggs, beaten
2 cups milk
½ cup oil
½ quart blueberries (2 cups)

Preheat oven to 400 degrees. Combine flour, corn meal, baking powder, salt and sugar in a large bowl. In a separate, smaller bowl mix the eggs, milk and oil. Mix the smaller bowl into the larger bowl until just moistened. Fold in the blueberries. Spoon into greased muffin tins and bake at 400 for twenty minutes.

Makes about two dozen.

Blueberry Muffins

Of course, these are best with fresh, Maine blueberries but any fresh blueberries will work as well. KJG

4 eggs, lightly beaten
½ cup butter, melted
1-pint (16 ounces) sour cream or yogurt
3-¾ cups flour
1-cup sugar
2 tablespoons plus two teaspoons baking powder
1-teaspoon salt
½ quart blueberries (2 cups)

Preheat oven to 400 degrees. Mix together the eggs, butter and sour cream or yogurt in a small bowl. Combine flour, sugar, baking powder and salt in a separate large bowl. Add the egg mixture to the large bowl. Mix until just combined and then add the blueberries. Batter will be lumpy. Spoon into greased muffin tins and bake for 20 minutes at 400 degrees.

Makes about two dozen.

Bran/Raisin Muffins

These are lighter than most bran muffins. My children liked this lighter version. KJG

3 ½ cups flour
½ cup whole-wheat flour
¼ cup bran
2/3-cup sugar
6-tablespoons baking powder
2-teaspoons salt
2 eggs
1 ½ cups milk
1-cup oil
1-cup raisins

Preheat oven to 400 degrees. Combine flour, whole-wheat flour, bran, sugar, baking powder and salt in a large mixing bowl. In a separate bowl, beat together eggs, milk, and oil. Pour the wet mixture into the dry ingredients and stir until just combined. Do not over mix. Fold in the raisins and spoon into greased muffin tins. Bake at 400 degrees for 20 minutes.

Makes about two dozen muffins.

Doughnut Muffins

These lighter, sweet muffins rise very nicely. KJG

4 ½ cups flour
2 tablespoons baking powder
1 ½ teaspoons salt
1 ½ teaspoons nutmeg
1 ½ cups sugar
1-cup oil
1 ½ cups milk
3 eggs
Cinnamon and sugar for sprinkling

Preheat oven to 400 degrees. Prepare muffin tins.
Measure the flour, baking powder, salt, nutmeg and sugar into
a large bowl. Mix well. In a separate bowl, mix the oil, milk
and eggs until well blended. Add the oil and milk mixture into
the flour mixture. Mix until just combined. Spoon into
prepared muffin tins. Sprinkle cinnamon and sugar mixture on
top of the muffins. Bake for 20 minutes or until inserted
toothpick comes out clean.

Makes approximately two dozen generous- sized muffins.

Gingerbread Muffins

3 cups flour
1 ½ teaspoons baking soda
1-teaspoon cinnamon
¼ teaspoon allspice
1-teaspoon ginger
½ teaspoon salt
1-cup butter (2 sticks)
½ cup brown sugar
2 eggs
¼ cup molasses
1-cup hot water

Preheat oven to 400 degrees. Mix together flour, baking soda, cinnamon, allspice, ginger and salt in a large bowl. In a separate bowl, mix the butter, sugar, eggs and molasses. Add the butter mixture to the flour mixture. Stir. Add the hot water and mix until just combined. Fill greased muffin tins about 2/3 full. These will crown nicely. Bake at 400 degrees for about twenty minutes.

Makes about 1 ½ dozen.

Maple Bran Muffins
There is a very filling muffin. KP

1 ¼ cup maple syrup
3 eggs
3 ¼ cups crushed bran flakes
1 ½ cups sour cream
1-½ cups flour
1 ½ teaspoons baking soda

Preheat oven to 400 degrees. Beat syrup and eggs together in a large bowl until well blended. Mix in the bran flakes and let stand a few minutes. In the meantime, in a separate bowl mix together flour and baking soda. Add the sour cream to the bran flakes and mix well. Add the flour minute to the bran mixture and stir just until moistened. Batter will be lumpy. Spoon into greased muffin tins. Bake at 400 degrees for about twenty minutes.

Orange-Chocolate Muffins

These muffins look great and smell heavenly. KP

2 cups flour
½ cup sugar
1-tablespoon baking powder
½ teaspoon salt
2 eggs, beaten
¾ cups orange juice
1/3-cup butter, melted
2 ounces semi-sweet chocolate, melted
grated rind of one orange

Preheat oven to 400 degrees. Combine the flour, sugar, baking powder, and salt in a large bowl. In a separate bowl, combine the eggs, orange juice and melted butter. Add the mixture to the larger bowl and combine until just mixed. Divide the batter into two separate bowls. Add the melted chocolate to one of the bowls, and the grated orange rind to the other bowl. Tip the muffin pans and spoon in orange batter first. Tip the pans the other way and spoon in chocolate batter. Bake at 400 degrees for approximately 20 minutes.

Makes 2 dozen

Not enough time to make these? Try this variation instead: Follow the above directions except omit the melted chocolate and do not divide the batter in half. Add 1 ½ cups mini-chocolate chips to the muffin batter along with the orange zest and spoon the batter into greased muffin tins. You get the same chocolate/orange flavor with less work!

Orange Poppyseed Muffins

2 cups flour
½ cup sugar
2 teaspoons baking powder
½ teaspoon baking soda
½ teaspoon salt
2/3 cups orange juice
½ cup oil
1 egg, beaten
grated zest of one orange
¼ cup poppy seeds

Preheat the oven to 400 degrees. Combine flour, sugar, baking powder, baking soda, and salt in a large bowl. In a separate, smaller bowl combine the orange juice, oil, egg, and grated zest. Add the mixture from the smaller bowl into the larger bowl and mix until just combined. Stir in poppy seeds. Spoon into greased muffin tins and bake at 400 for approximately 20 minutes.

Makes about 1-½ dozen muffins.

Pumpkin Cranberry Muffins

2 ½ cups flour
1 ½ cups sugar
2-½ teaspoons baking powder
1-teaspoon baking soda
¾ teaspoon cinnamon
¼ teaspoon cloves
¼ teaspoon nutmeg
½ cup oil
½ cup orange juice
½ can (15 ounces) pumpkin or squash
1 egg, beaten
1-cup milk
½ cup cranberry raisins (optional)

Preheat the oven to 400 degrees. Combine the flour, sugar, baking powder, soda, cinnamon, cloves and nutmeg in a large bowl. In a separate bowl, mix the oil, orange juice, pumpkin, eggs and milk. Add the mixture from the smaller bowl to the larger bowl; mix until just combined. Fold in the cranberry raisins. Spoon into greased muffin tins and bake at 400 degrees for about 20 minutes.

Makes two dozen.

Rhubarb Maple Muffins

1-½ cups diced rhubarb
½ cup packed brown sugar
2 ¼ cups flour
1-tablespoon baking powder
½ teaspoon salt
2 teaspoons cinnamon
½ teaspoon nutmeg
½ cup butter
1 egg
½ cup maple syrup
2/3-cup milk
zest of one lemon

Preheat oven to 400 degrees. Mix together rhubarb and brown sugar – set aside for at least 45 minutes. Combine the flour, baking powder, salt, cinnamon, and nutmeg in a large bowl. In a separate bowl, mix the butter, egg and maple syrup. Alternating with the milk, add the ingredients from the smaller bowl into the large, combining until just mixed. Fold in the rhubarb and lemon zest. Spoon into greased muffin tins and bake at 400 degrees for about 20 minutes.

Makes about 1 ½ dozen.

Breakfast

Breakfast

As if the muffins weren't enough, you then can enjoy wonderful "real" breakfast foods like the Lewis R. French Toast.

Cinnamon Rolls

Cinnamon Mixture:
½ cup butter (1 stick), melted
1/3-cup brown sugar
1-tablespoon cinnamon

Mix ingredients in a small mixing bowl and place to the side.

Dough:
3 ½ teaspoons yeast
¾ cup warm water
¾ cup milk, scaled, then cooled
½ cup sugar
½ cup butter or shortening (1 stick), softened
1 ½ teaspoon salt
2 eggs
4-6 cups flour

Preheat oven to 375 degrees. Sprinkle the yeast over the warm water and let sit in a warm place for about 5 minutes. Stir in milk, sugar, butter, salt, eggs and about 2-3 cups of flour. Beat until smooth. Mix in enough flour to make dough that is easy to handle. Continue kneading in large bowl until the dough is smooth and elastic. Cover and let rise in a warm place until double. Punch down, divide into two pieces. Roll out each piece into rectangles; spread with cinnamon mixture, roll up and place seam side down in brownie pans. You can also use loaf pans if you desire. Cut with scissors, not quite through the roll, to make ten-twelve sections. Gently pull the sections so that they will rise and bake apart from each other. Let rise again and then bake until golden brown on top – about 20-25 minutes. Drizzle the glaze over top and serve in the pan.

Glaze:
1 cup powdered sugar
2-3 tablespoons milk
½ teaspoon vanilla
grated orange peel or orange juice or both (optional)

Mix all of the ingredients together until you have a consistency that you like. Add more milk or powdered sugar if necessary. Pour over cooling cinnamon rolls.

Lewis R. French Toast

12 eggs
1-2 cups milk
¾ cup water
1-teaspoon vanilla
¼ teaspoon nutmeg
¼ teaspoon almond extract
12 slices bread

Combine all the ingredients except the bread in a large mixing bowl. Dip bread piece- by- piece, coating both sides. Fry on hot greased griddle or frying pan. Keep warm until served.

Serves 6-8.

Orange Poppyseed Pancakes

This batter is thicker than sour cream pancakes and rises nicely on the griddle. KP

2 ½ cups flour
1-teaspoon salt
1-½ teaspoons baking powder
3 eggs
1 ½ cups orange juice
¼ cup honey
¼ cup poppy seeds
¼ cup butter, melted

Dry whisk together the flour, salt, and baking powder in a large bowl. In a separate, smaller bowl, mix together eggs, orange juice and honey. Pour into dry mixture. Add melted butter and mix until just blended. Fold in poppy seeds. Cook on hot griddle or frying pan.

Sour Cream Blueberry Pancakes

3 ½ cups flour
2 tablespoons baking powder
½ teaspoon salt
2 tablespoons sugar
2 eggs
2 cups milk
½ cup sour cream
4 tablespoons butter, melted
1-cup blueberries

Mix together flour, baking powder, salt, and sugar in a large bowl. In separate bowls beat together eggs, milk, and sour cream. Pour into dry mixture and blend until just mixed. Add the butter and mix again until just mixed. Gently mix in berries. Pour pancakes onto hot, greased griddle until brown. Flip and cook other side.

Serves 6-8.

Lunch

Soups

Soups and salads are served for lunch on the Lewis R. French. The soups vary each day but all are filling and delicious. When the weather cooperates (or even on days that are rainy and the tarp keeps passengers dry) meals are served buffet style on deck. The informal setting makes for great eating. Ever notice how atmosphere adds to a meal? How can you not enjoy these fine soups with the beautiful Maine scenery in the background? But they are good enough to keep tummies happy at home as well. KJG

Brandied Pumpkin Soup

On the first day of our cruise the first mate told us we were having pumpkin soup for lunch. "Ugh," I thought. I'm not a big pumpkin fan and the soup didn't even sound good. Then I smelled it. "Yummy," I thought. And when I tasted it, I thought, "Double yummy!" I was delightfully surprised. This soup has a warm, rich taste and would be perfect in the autumn or for the first course at your Thanksgiving Dinner as well as for a light summer dinner or lunch. It is a thin soup. KJG

½ cup butter
2 to 3 onions, chopped
2 (15-ounce) cans plain pumpkin
8 cups chicken broth
1-teaspoon ground ginger
1-teaspoon nutmeg
1 ½ cups milk
1/3-cup brandy
Salt and pepper to taste
Croutons

Heat butter in soup pot and sauté onion until tender and transparent. Stir in pumpkin, broth, ginger and nutmeg. Blend well and bring to a boil. Reduce heat. About ½ hour before serving, add brandy and milk, and heat through. Do not let boil. Serve with croutons.

Serves 6 – 8.

Kathy's Corn Chowder

Use leftovers with chopped lobster for lobster chowder at brunch. KP

1-½ tablespoons butter
2 – 3 medium onions, chopped
2 – 3 stalks celery, chopped
1-teaspoon thyme
1 – 2 teaspoons basil
1 ½ teaspoon parsley
5 cups water or stock
2 – 3 pounds potatoes, peeled and chopped
4   (15 ¼ ounce) cans corn
2 (12 ounce) cans evaporated whole milk

Melt the butter in a large soup pot and sauté the onions and celery. Add thyme, basil and parsley. Add water or stock and potatoes, cover and cook until potatoes are tender. Add the canned corn about 45 minutes before serving. About 20 minutes before serving add milk and heat through but do not let boil.

Serves about 8 – 10.

Fish Chowder

3 medium onions, chopped
¼ cup (1/2 stick) butter
2 ½ pounds (6 to 8 medium) potatoes, peeled and diced
5 cups water or stock (fish, chicken, or vegetable)
2 tablespoons parsley
salt and pepper to taste
2 ½ pounds haddock, in one piece
1 can evaporated milk

In soup pot melt the butter and sauté onions until translucent.
Add potatoes, water or stock, parsley, salt and pepper and bring
to boil. Simmer, covered, until potatoes are tender. About 1/2
hour before serving add fish; do not cut fish up! Fifteen
minutes before serving, add the milk and heat through, but do
not boil.

Serves 6.

French Onion Soup

5 pounds onions
1-cup butter
salt and pepper to taste
beef broth*
1 cup brandy or dry sherry
Swiss cheese, grated
croutons

In large soup pot, sauté onions in butter until translucent. Add about 6 cups beef broth. Bring to a boil, cover and let simmer. Salt and pepper to taste. About one half-hour before serving add brandy or sherry. Serve with croutons and grated Swiss cheese.

Serves 6.

*You can make this vegetarian by using Better than Bouillon Mushroom Base for broth instead of beef.

Garlic Soup

This soup is thin and very mild with a nutty flavor. Leftovers make a great chicken or turkey soup base. KP

16 ounce jar (approximately 1 ¾ cups) minced garlic
¼ cup peanut oil or canola oil
2 quarts (8 cups) water (or light vegetable stock), more if needed
¼ cup soy sauce
½ medium green cabbage, shredded
4-5 carrots, cut 1"
2 stalks celery, chopped
2-3 mushrooms, sliced (optional)
crushed red pepper

Sauté garlic in oil until it starts to brown. Add all the remaining ingredients, bring to a boil. Simmer, covered, until vegetables are tender. Sprinkle lightly with red pepper flakes, let passengers (or guests) garnish with more if they want.

Serves 6.

Italian Sausage Soup

I made this for a gathering for friends moving out of state.
Everyone loved this unusual soup and had seconds. KJG

2-3 pounds sweet or hot Italian sausage
6 cloves of minced garlic (1/4 cup)
2 large onions, chopped
2 cans (28 ounces) Italian style tomatoes
3 cans beef stock (about 4-5 cups broth/bouillon)
½ cup dry red wine
4 tablespoons fresh parsley, minced
3 teaspoons basil
1-2 bell peppers, chopped
2 small zucchini, chopped
1 (one pound) package uncooked bow tie pasta
Grated Parmesan cheese

Remove and discard the casings from the sausage and break
meat up into pieces. In soup pot, sauté sausage, garlic, and
onions in a small amount of stock until sausage is browned.
Turn contents of pot into colander to drain out grease. Rinse
and return to the soup pot. Add tomatoes, stock, wine, parsley
and basil. Simmer for 45 minutes or so, stirring occasionally.
Add zucchini and bell peppers. Simmer for about 20 minutes.
About 30 minutes before serving stir in pasta and cook until
just tender.

Serve with Parmesan cheese.

Serves 6 – 8.

Lentil, Spinach and Squash Soup

This soup is thick and spicy. Goes well with corn bread! KP

4 tablespoons oil
2 medium onions, chopped
2 slices (1 ½" thick) fresh ginger
¼ cup minced garlic
2 teaspoons ground cumin
2 teaspoons turmeric
1-teaspoon coriander
1-teaspoon red pepper
1 ½ cups uncooked lentils
2 yellow squash or zucchini or mixture of both, cut into ½" rounds
5   cups chicken (or vegetable) stock
2 packages frozen, chopped spinach – thawed and squeezed dry
1 16-ounce can whole tomatoes, chopped (reserve juice)
Sour cream or plain yogurt

Heat oil in large soup pot. Add onions, ginger, garlic, cumin, turmeric, coriander, and red pepper. Cook until the onions are soft. Mix in lentils, squash and spinach. Add stock, tomatoes, and the reserved juice. Bring to a boil; reduce heat and simmer, stirring occasionally.

Serve with a dollop of sour cream or yogurt.

Serves 6-8.

Potato Leek Cheese Soup

3 cups diced potatoes (about 4 pounds or 12 medium)
2 cups water or vegetable stock
1 leek, sliced thinly
1-tablespoon oil
parsley
2 cups milk
1 cup shredded Cheddar cheese
2 tablespoons butter
½ teaspoon salt
ground black pepper
pinch garlic powder

In large pot, cook the potatoes in the water until tender. Drain, reserving cooking liquid. In large skillet sauté leek slices in the oil until soft. Mash a portion of the potatoes in the soup pot with the liquid, leeks, and parsley. Whisk until as smooth as you can make it. Add milk. Stirring often, add cheese, butter, salt, pepper, and garlic powder. Heat until cheese is melted and soup is hot. Do not let the soup boil after milk and cheese are added.

Serves 6.

Spicy Black Bean Soup
Goes well with corn bread. KP

½ package one pound bacon (about 8 – 9 slices), diced
1-2 large onions, chopped
1-tablespoon garlic, minced
3-4 carrots, peeled and chopped small
2-3 sticks celery, chopped small
3-4 jalapeno peppers, stemmed, seeded, and diced
¼ cup ground cumin
1/3-cup oregano
one package black turtle beans, soaked overnight*
6 cups chicken or vegetable stock
¾ cup lime juice (1/2 bottle lime juice or 6-8 medium limes)
¾ cup cream sherry
¾ cup fresh cilantro, minced (or 2 teaspoons dried cilantro)
Sour cream for garnish

*Make sure to soak beans overnight. Cover with water and soak. Precook in early morning 1-2 hours, adding more water if necessary, drain.

Cook bacon until crisp in a large soup pot. Remove to drain on paper towels. Add onion, garlic, carrots, and celery to bacon fat and sauté. Add jalapenos and cook until tender, five minutes or so. Stir in cumin and oregano.

Add black beans and stock. Simmer uncovered until beans are very tender. Stir in lime juice, sherry, and bacon. Just before serving add cilantro. Serve sour cream on the side for topping.

Serves 6 – 8.

Tomato Soup

2 ½ cups chopped onions (3-4 onions)
¼ cup minced garlic
¼ cup (1/2 stick) butter
¼ cup olive oil
4 medium tomatoes, chopped
1-tablespoon dill weed
salt and pepper to taste
2 cans (32 oz) crushed tomatoes
¼ cup honey
¼ cup mayonnaise or sour cream (room temperature)

Sauté onions and garlic in butter and olive oil. Add chopped
tomatoes and dill. Add salt and pepper to taste. Next, add
canned tomatoes, honey, and water if needed. Let simmer.

One half hour before serving, add the mayonnaise or sour
cream. Heat through but do not let boil.

Serves 6.

Kathy's Vegetable Soup

This is a great way to use up leftover vegetables! KP

2 large cans V-8 vegetable juice
2 medium onions studded with whole cloves (not too many per onion)
1-teaspoon basil
2 tablespoons garlic, minced
vegetables: carrots, onions, celery, peppers, potatoes, squash, beans, and any other leftover vegetables or undressed salad (chopped)

(You can add leftover breakfast sausage or cooked hamburger meat too).

Pour the V-8 juice into large soup pot. Add studded onions and basil. Add any uncooked vegetables right away. About a half-hour before serving add any cooked vegetables.

Serves 8-10.

Rob's Vegetarian Chili

This also goes well with corn bread and is another excellent recipe to add any leftover vegetables to! KP

1-cup olive oil
1 –2 zucchini, diced
3 onions, chopped
¼ -cup garlic, minced
1 – 2 large red peppers, diced
1-½ teaspoons salt
2 pounds plum tomatoes, diced (about 6)
2 cans (10.5 oz) plum tomatoes and juice
3 tablespoons chili powder
1-tablespoon cumin
1 – 2 tablespoons basil
1 – 2 tablespoons oregano
1 tablespoon ground black pepper
parsley
1 can kidney beans, drained
1 can chickpeas, drained
1-tablespoon dill weed
¼ cup lemon or lime juice
toppings on the side: Monterey jack cheese, shredded; sour cream or yogurt

Sauté zucchini, onions, peppers, and garlic in olive oil.
Combine this with all other ingredients in soup kettle. Simmer uncovered. Serve with toppings.

Serves 6-8.

Salads and Dressings

Here are the salads to go with your soups. Some are simple salads and there are lots of dressings to top your favorite greens. KJG

Caesar Salad

1 head romaine lettuce
½ teaspoon garlic, minced
1 coddled egg*
croutons
¼ cup grated Parmesan cheese
1 lemon, cut in half

Dressing:
1/3-cup olive oil
1 teaspoon Worcestershire sauce
½ teaspoon salt
½ teaspoon dry mustard
fresh ground pepper

Rub the salad bowl with the garlic. Allow some to remain in the bowl and add the rest to the dressing. Tear lettuce into pieces. Mix the dressing, and pour over the lettuce until the leaves glisten. Break the coddled egg into the salad, squeeze the lemon all over and toss again. Just before serving, add the croutons and the cheese.

*Coddled eggs (do ahead of time) – Place cold egg in warm water in a small bowl. Heat some water in a saucepan until boiling. Gently immerse the egg into the boiling water. Remove pot from heat, and let stand about three minutes. Immediately cool egg in cold water and keep chilled until use.

Serves 6-8.

Cool Cucumber Salad

3 large cucumbers
1-teaspoon salt
1 tablespoon white wine vinegar
1 tablespoon plus 1 teaspoon olive oil
2 radishes or one small sweet onion, sliced thinly
1 ½ cup plain yogurt

Mix together vinegar and olive oil. Place cucumbers and radishes or onions in salad bowl. Pour vinegar/olive oil mixture over vegetables and let salad marinade at least an hour. Add yogurt about fifteen minutes before serving.

Serves 4-6.

Chinese Cabbage Salad

1 head Napa cabbage
½ cup scallions, sliced
½ cup slivered almonds, toasted
1 can chow mein noodles

Dressing:
2 tablespoons sugar
¼ cup light oil
2 tablespoons rice wine vinegar
1 ½ teaspoons soy sauce

Toast the almonds in dry frying pan. Set aside until needed.
Cut cabbage into bite-sized pieces. Toss with scallions in salad
bowl. Add dressing and allow to marinate about ½ hour or so.
Just before serving, add almonds and chow mein noodles and
toss again.

Creamy Mustard Dressing

¾ cup mayonnaise
3 tablespoons Half & Half
2 teaspoons dry mustard
¾ teaspoon salt
3/8-teaspoon ground pepper

Mix all together and serve over tossed salad.

Coleslaw Dressing

1-cup sour cream
½ cup mayonnaise
1 teaspoon dry mustard
1 teaspoon seasoned salt
¼ teaspoon ground pepper

Mix all ingredients and serve over shredded cabbage for coleslaw.

French Dressing

1-cup olive or vegetable oil
¼ cup white vinegar
¼ cup lemon juice
1-teaspoon salt
1 teaspoon dry mustard
½ teaspoon paprika

Mix all ingredients together.

Italian Dressing

1-cup vegetable oil
¼ cup lemon juice
¼ cup white vinegar
1-teaspoon salt
1-teaspoon sugar
1-teaspoon dry mustard
½ teaspoon onion powder
½ teaspoon paprika
½ teaspoon oregano
1/8-teaspoon thyme
1-teaspoon garlic, minced

Mix all ingredients and chill.

Russian Dressing

1-cup mayonnaise
½ cup chili sauce
1 tablespoon minced onion
1 teaspoon lemon juice

Mix all ingredients and chill.

Spinach Salad

2 cups spinach
1 head romaine lettuce
½ pound bacon (8 – 9 slices), cooked and crumbled
1 bunch scallions, sliced thin
1-cup mushrooms, sliced

Dressing:
2 tablespoons lemon juice
½ cup olive oil
1-teaspoon salt
1- teaspoon pepper
½ teaspoon dry mustard
¼ teaspoon sugar
1 egg yolk

A few hours before serving: slice mushrooms into small mixing bowl, mix together dressing ingredients and pour over the mushrooms. Marinate for several hours. Stir when you think about it. Just before serving, toss everything together.

Sweet & Sour Dressing

¾ cup vegetable oil
1/3-cup rice vinegar
1/3-cup sugar
3 tablespoons snipped parsley (or one tablespoon dried)
1 ½ teaspoon salt
pepper to taste
¾ dashes of Tabasco sauce

Mix all ingredients and chill.

Thousand Island Dressing

1-cup mayonnaise
2 tablespoons chili sauce
2 tablespoons stuffed green olives, chopped
2 teaspoons chives
½ teaspoon paprika
1 hard egg, chopped

Mix all ingredients and chill.

Breads

Delicious homemade breads are served every day on the boat. Paired with the soups and a tossed salad, they make a complete meal.

Anadama Bread

This bread is not for times when you are in a hurry. When Kathy told me that it rises three times, I was surprised – but it is well worth it! KJG

¼ cup (1/2 stick) butter
½ cup molasses
½ cup cornmeal
1 ½ cup water
¼ cup warm water
1-tablespoon yeast
½ teaspoon baking soda
5 –6 cups flour

In small saucepan combine butter, molasses, cornmeal, and water. Stir constantly to keep cornmeal from clumping. Cook until thick. Remove from heat and cool to lukewarm. Dissolve the yeast in the warm water. Pour into large glass bowl. Add lukewarm cornmeal mixture and enough flour to make a stiff dough, springy and not sticky. Put in a warm place and let rise until double. Punch down, let rise again. Shape into two loaves, and let rise again. Bake at 350 degrees for about 30 – 35 minutes.

Makes two loaves.

Cheese & Garlic Muffins

These are categorized as bread instead of muffins because they are more a dinner roll than a breakfast muffin.   KJG

4 1/3 cups flour
2/3-cups sugar
2 tablespoons plus ¼ teaspoon baking powder
1 ½ teaspoons onion powder
2 eggs
1 1/3 cups milk
¾ cups oil
1-tablespoon garlic, minced
1-¼ cups shredded cheddar cheese

Preheat the oven to 400 degrees. Combine flour, sugar, baking powder, and onion powder in a large mixing bowl, make a well in the center. In a smaller bowl, mix the eggs, milk and oil, mixing thoroughly. Pour the wet mixture into the dry mixture, blend until just mixed. Do not over mix. Mix in garlic and cheddar cheese. Spoon into greased muffin tins.

Makes about two dozen.

Corn Bread

This corn bread is simply the best in the world. My southern boy – a real cornbread connoisseur – had four pieces the day this was served for lunch. Make sure that you bake your cornbread in a cast iron skillet. It wouldn't be as good if you didn't. KJG

This is one of my most requested recipes. KP

1-½ cups flour
2-¼ cups cornmeal
1 ½ teaspoons baking soda
¾ teaspoon salt
3 eggs
¾ cup brown sugar (not packed)
2-¼ cups buttermilk
¾ cups butter, melted (1 ½ sticks)

Preheat oven to 400 degrees. Combine the flour, cornmeal, baking soda and salt in a large bowl. In a separate bowl, mix the eggs and brown sugar until light and fluffy. Add the buttermilk and mix well. Add the dry mixture to the buttermilk mixture. Mix gently until just blended. Melt butter in a small saucepan. Dip paper towel into the butter and thoroughly coat preheated 12-inch cast-iron skillet. Add the rest of the butter to the corn bread mix, blending until just mixed. Pour the batter into the frying pan and bake in preheated over for 30 to 35 minutes until golden brown.

Makes one 12-inch skillet full.

Dill Cottage Cheese Bread

2 tablespoons yeast
½ cup warm water
¼ cup sugar
2 tablespoons minced onion
2 cups cottage cheese, at room temperature
¼ cup (1/2 stick) butter, melted
½ teaspoon baking soda
2 tablespoons plus 1-teaspoon dill weed
2 teaspoons salt
2 eggs
about 5 cups flour

Dissolve yeast in warm water and let it sit for a few minutes. Combine sugar, onion, cottage cheese, butter, baking soda, dill weed, salt and eggs in a large bowl and mix well. Add the yeast mixture. Add enough flour to make a stiff dough. Let it rise until double. Punch down, shape into loaves or rolls, and let rise again. Bake at 375 degrees for 35 minutes.

Makes two loaves.

Italian Bread

Try adding garlic, onions, Parmesan cheese, basil, oregano, and parsley for a festive look and really good Italian flavor. KP

2 tablespoons yeast
2 ½ cups warm water
1-tablespoon salt
6 – 7 cups flour

Dissolve yeast in the warm water and let it sit a few minutes. Combine yeast mixture with five cups of the flour and salt in a large ceramic bowl, mixing well. Add enough of the remaining flour to make a stiff dough. Cover and let rise until double. Shape into loaves, and let rise again. Bake at 400 degrees for 25 minutes.

Makes two large loaves.

Leftover Oatmeal Bread

Most of us don't have that much leftover oatmeal, but then again, most of us don't pilot a boat with 24 people! Kathy said this bread is soft and delicate and goes well with everything.
KJG

1-tablespoon yeast
¾ cup warm water
1-tablespoon sugar
2-½ teaspoons salt
2 cups cooked oatmeal (or cooked rice, or cooked barley)
1/4-cup oil
4 – 5 cups flour

Dissolve yeast in the warm water and let set a few minutes. In large ceramic bowl, mix five cups of the flour, sugar, salt, oil, and oatmeal. Add yeast mixture, and add more water if the dough is too dry at this stage. Add in enough flour to make a firm, springy dough. Cover and let rise until double. Shape into loaves, let rise again, and bake at 375 for 30 minutes.

Makes two smallish loaves.

Potato Rolls

Makes a nice dinner roll. KP

1 cup russet potato, peeled, boiled and well mashed
1-cup warm water
½ cup sugar
1-½ tablespoons yeast
4 – 5 cups flour
3 eggs .
½ cup (1 stick) butter, melted
1-teaspoon salt

Place mashed potato, water, sugar and yeast in a large ceramic bowl. Whisk well. Add 2 cups of the flour, and whisk until smooth. Add one more cup of flour, whisk until smooth. Cover, and let rise until double.

Add the eggs one at a time, mixing after each one. Add butter and salt, blend together. Add enough remaining flour to make a stiff dough that doesn't stick. Shape into balls, and place in greased muffin tins. Let rise again until double.

Bake at 375 for 15 – 20 minutes until golden gold brown and puffy.

Rye Bread with Applesauce and Cheese

This makes heavy but very tasty bread. Goes well with onion soup. KP

2 cups rye flour
6 – 9 cups flour
3 tablespoons yeast
3 ½ cups shredded sharp cheddar cheese
4 teaspoons salt
3 cups applesauce
½ cup dark molasses
½ cup butter (1 stick)

Combine the rye flour, 4 cups of the regular flour, yeast, cheddar, and salt in a large ceramic bowl. Heat the applesauce, molasses and butter in a medium saucepan until the butter melts. Add warm mixture to flour mixture and mix well. Add enough flour to make a stiff dough. Let rise until double (this bread takes its time rising). Punch down, shape into leaves, and let rise again.

Bake at 350 degrees for 25 minutes.

Makes four smallish loaves.

Whole Wheat Bread

2-¾ cups water
½ cup brown sugar
¼ cup (1/2 stick) shortening or butter
2 tablespoons yeast
5 cups flour
3 cups whole-wheat flour

Put water, sugar, and shortening into a small saucepan and heat until just warm. In a large ceramic bowl, mix 3 cups flour and yeast. Add the warmed liquid mixture and the whole-wheat flour. Add in enough remaining flour to make a firm dough. Cover and let rise until double. Shape into loaves, and let rise again. Bake at 375 for 30 minutes.

Makes two loaves.

Yogurt Pumpernickel Bread

I think this is my overall favorite bread. It is light brown color and very tasty. It goes well with chowders or other somewhat blander soups. KP

2 ¼ teaspoons yeast (one package)
1-teaspoon brown sugar
1-cup warm water
1 tablespoon unsweetened cocoa powder
1-tablespoon salt
½ cup bran
1-cup whole-wheat flour
1 ½ cups rye flour
2 cups plain yogurt
¼ cup butter, melted (1/2 stick)
3-4 cups flour

Preheat oven to 350 degrees. Spray two loaf pans with non-stick spray. You can also shape it round and bake on a greased cookie sheet. In a small mixing bowl, combine the yeast and sugar with the water. Stir to dissolve the yeast and sugar and let it stand until foamy – be careful or it may overflow if unwatched – about 10 minutes. In a large bowl, combine the cocoa, salt, bran, whole-wheat flour, and rye flour. Add the yogurt, butter, and then the yeast mixture. Beat hard for about one minute. Add flour until a soft dough forms. Keep adding until slightly tacky and springs back when touched. Cover and let rise in a warm place until double. Form loaves and let rise again. Bake in preheated oven about 30 – 40 minutes. Bread will have a hollow sound when tapped.

Makes two loaves.

Appetizers

Appetizers

Every afternoon, the chef would bring up an appetizer to "wet" our appetites. These are also great for parties and snacks. KJG

Dill Dip

1 ½ cups mayonnaise
1-cup sour cream
½ cup plain yogurt
2 teaspoons Beau Monde or Lawry's Seasoned salt
3 tablespoons dill weed

Combine all the ingredients. Let chill for at least one hour before serving. The longer this one sits the better the flavor.

Guacamole Dip

3 avocados, pitted and peeled
2 scallions, trimmed and sliced thin
1-teaspoon garlic, minced
2 tablespoons lemon juice
2 small plum tomatoes, coarsely chopped
1 small handfuls of cilantro leaves, minced (or one tablespoon dried)
¼ teaspoon cayenne pepper
Salt to taste

Mash avocados with a fork until coarsely pureed. Add scallions, garlic, lemon juice and tomatoes and mix. Add cilantro. Season with cayenne pepper and salt to taste.
Let sit, covered at room temperature for about 30 minutes for spices to blend before serving.

Serves 6-8.

Herbed Cream Cheese Dip

12 ounces cream cheese
1/3 cup grated Parmesan cheese
1 tablespoon plus 1-½ teaspoons garlic powder
1 ½ teaspoons lemon juice
1-2 dashes Tabasco sauce
1 – 2 dashes Worcestershire sauce
1 tablespoon chopped onion
1-½ teaspoons whole celery seeds
1/3 cup chopped fresh chives
salt and pepper to taste

Mix all ingredients until well blended. Chill before serving.

Serves 6-8.

Lobster Dip

1-cup lobster meat, chopped
1   8-ounce package cream cheese, softened
¼ teaspoon garlic powder
½ cup mayonnaise
1 teaspoon powdered mustard
1 tablespoon lemon juice
1 tablespoon minced onion
Salt to taste

Mix together all ingredients and chill until use.

Serves 6- 8.

Olive Dip

12 ounces cream cheese, softened
Milk or Half- &-Half to thin out the cheese
¼ to ½ cup green olives, chopped
1-teaspoon garlic powder

Combine the cream cheese and milk to make a dip consistency.
Mix in garlic powder and olives. Let dip chill for at least one
hour for maximum flavor. Thin with more milk if too thick.

Serves 6-8.

Whit's Dip

1-cup mayonnaise
1 cup grated onion
1 cup grated cheese (Cheddar, Swiss or combination)

Bake at 350 degrees. Mix together in baking dishes and bake until brown and bubbly.

Supper

Supper

Supper is always special on the Lewis R. French. The day is coming to an end and the gathering to eat on the deck is peaceful and satisfying. KJG

Apricot Bourbon Chicken

This chicken is simply delicious. It is easy enough to make for a quick weekday dinner but fancy enough for company. If you can't find chutney, use a whole jar of apricot jam. It will still be great. KJG

3 pounds chicken breast, boneless and skinless
2-3 onions, chopped
1-tablespoon garlic, minced
¼ cup butter
½ jar (8 ounce) chutney
½ jar (8 ounce) apricot jam
1-cup bourbon (whiskey)

Sauté onions and garlic in the butter. Add the chutney, jam and bourbon. Mix well.   Place the chicken in a lasagna pan and smother with the sautéed mixture. Cover with foil and bake about 35 minutes in a 350-degree oven. We also made this with pheasant and it worked equally well and was delicious.

Serves 6 – 8.

Chicken Dijonaise

3 pounds chicken breast, boneless, skinless, cut into bite-sized pieces
1/3 cup Dijon mustard
salt and pepper
olive oil
1/3 cup butter, divided into two equal parts
3 tablespoons flour
2 cups dry white wine
3 bay leaves
3 tablespoons fresh rosemary, crushed (or 2 tablespoons dried rosemary – not ground)

Sprinkle the chicken with salt and pepper and coat with mustard. Heat oil and half the butter in large frying pan and brown meat on all sides. Put the chicken in large baking pan. Tuck in bay leaves and sprinkle with rosemary evenly. Add flour and the rest of the butter to the frying pan, whisk in wine, blending well. Pour over evenly over chicken. Add more water, wine, or chicken stock so that the chicken is ¾ immersed in liquid. Cover pan with foil and bake for about 45 minutes at 350 degrees.

Serves 6-8.

Kathy's Crumb-Dilly Fish

3 pounds haddock
1 carrot, chopped fine
1 onion, minced
1 stalk celery, chopped fine
1-tablespoon garlic, minced
1-cup breadcrumbs (or more)
olive oil
½ cup mayonnaise
1/3-cup sour cream
¼ cup plain yogurt
1-tablespoon dill weed
1 tablespoon lemon juice
dry white wine (or chicken stock or water)

Sauté carrot, onion, celery and garlic in olive oil until the onion is translucent and vegetables are a little soft. Add breadcrumbs. Mix until brown and crumbly, adding more olive oil if too dry. Remove from heat. Mix together the mayonnaise, sour cream, yogurt and dill. (This can be done ahead of time.) Lay fish in large pan. Spread dill dip mixture evenly over fish then coat evenly with bread crumb/vegetable mixture. Pour in wine until liquid is about ½ inch at bottom of pan. Add lemon juice evenly. Bake at 350 until fish is flaky and tender and top is brown, about 30 minutes.

Serves 6-8.

Lemon Chicken

3 pounds chicken, boneless, skinless, cut into bite-sized pieces
1-cup flour
salt and pepper
1 onion, chopped
2 tablespoons garlic, minced
olive oil
1 cup dry white wine or dry vermouth
2 cups chicken stock
2 lemons, thinly sliced

Mix together chicken, flour, salt and pepper in a large bowl. Sauté the onions and garlic in olive oil. Brown the chicken with sautéed onions and garlic, adding olive oil as necessary. Scrape up the brown residue off the bottom of the pan from time to time. Put the chicken and sautéed mixture in large pan and add wine and chicken stock. Cover the chicken with sliced lemons, cover pan with foil and bake about 40 minutes at 350 degrees.

Serves 6- 8.

Merrill's Easy-Cheesy Fish

3 pounds haddock
¼ cup mayonnaise
½ cup container Parmesan cheese
1-cup breadcrumbs

Lay out fish in lasagna pans. In medium bowl, mix together mayonnaise and Parmesan cheese until it's a thick paste. Add more cheese if necessary. Spread evenly over the fish. Sprinkle breadcrumbs over all to coat evenly. Bake until fish is flaky tender and the top is brown – about 30 minutes at 350 degrees.

Serves 6-8.

Paprika Chicken

2-3 pounds boneless, skinless chicken, cut up
1-cup flour
1 tablespoon Hungarian (sweet) paprika
1/2-teaspoon basil
¼ cup olive oil
1 teaspoon minced garlic
¼ cup Worcestershire sauce*
½ cup dry white wine
1-cup sour cream

Mix the flour, paprika and basil in a bag. Add chicken pieces
and shake to coat evenly. Heat oil in skillet. Brown chicken
and garlic. Mix together the wine and Worcestershire sauce.
Pour over chicken. Cover and simmer on low until chicken is
very tender (30-45 minutes). Set sour cream out to warm
to room temperature. Remove chicken when done. Blend in
sour cream. Heat until warmed through. Don't let it boil. Serve
with rice.

*White wine variety if you have it. If not, it'll just be a little
spicier, which is also good.

Serves 6-8.

Pork Loin with Coriander and Garlic

2-3 pounds boneless pork tenderloin (best if in one to two pound pieces)
1 jar ground coriander (1.7 ounces/48 grams)
¼ cup garlic, minced
1 ½ cups breadcrumbs
¼ cup olive oil

Preheat oven to 350 degrees. Mix together coriander, garlic, breadcrumbs, and olive oil to make a thick paste. You need to smell the coriander, see the garlic, and have it thick enough to hold its consistency when pressing onto the pork, not too dry, not too wet. Adjust ingredients as necessary. Arrange the tenderloins in a 9" x 13" pan. Press the paste mixture firmly and evenly on all sides of pork. Bake until the pork is just done. (Internal temperature of meat is 145 – 150 degrees. Use an instant meat thermometer) and remove from the oven. You can use this recipe with thick boneless pork chops, too.

Serves 6-8.

Simply Savory Baked Fish

3-4 pounds haddock
1 ½ cups breadcrumbs
1 stick butter
1/3-cup cider vinegar
1/3 cup Worcestershire sauce
1/3 cup lemon juice
¼ cup Dijon mustard

Preheat oven to 350 degrees. Dredge the fish through the breadcrumbs and place in 9" x 13" pan. Melt butter in medium saucepan. Stir in vinegar, Worcestershire sauce, lemon juice, and mustard. Pour mixture evenly over fish. Bake until fish is flaky and tender about 30 minutes. Cover if it starts to burn before done.

Serves 6.

Desserts

Desserts and Snacks to "tide" you over

*Don't plan on losing weight on a cruise on the Lewis R.
French. Delicious desserts tempt passengers every day and
after dinner. These cookies and other desserts will please the
fussiest of passengers.*

*In addition to the sweets, there were other delicious snacks as
well. Even though you would think that you couldn't eat
anything else, you would find room! I noticed there were never
any leftovers at the end of the day. KJG*

Absolutely Decadent Rice Krispie Bars
These are very rich. KP

1 cup light corn syrup
1 cup sugar
1 ½ cups peanut butter
1 teaspoon vanilla
6 cups Rice Krispies
6 ounces (1 cup) chocolate chips
6 ounces (1 cup) butterscotch chips

In large saucepan combine corn syrup and sugar. Cook over medium heat until sugar is melted. Do not overcook or sugar will crystallize! Remove from heat and pour into large mixing bowl containing peanut butter and vanilla. Mix together until smooth. Add Rice Krispies (if you spray the spoon with food release spray, nothing sticks as much to the spoon so you can mix it together better) and combine thoroughly.

Press mixture into greased 11" x 7" pan. Set aside to cool and harden.

Mix together chocolate chips and butterscotch chips and allow to melt on bun warmer. (If you melt them on the stove, watch them carefully, stirring constantly so they don't burn.) Pour evenly over bars, spreading as necessary, and place pan in fridge until serving time.

Best Ever Brownies

1 cup (2 sticks) butter or shortening, softened
4 eggs
2 cups sugar
2 teaspoons vanilla
1-½ cups flour
¾ cup cocoa
1-teaspoon salt
1-cup mini-chocolate chips

In large mixing bowl, combine shortening, eggs, sugar and vanilla. In a separate, smaller bowl dry whisk together flour, cocoa and salt. Pour dry mixture into wet mixture. Blend well. Fold in chocolate chips. Spread into greased brownie pans, and bake at 350 degrees for 30 minutes.

Carrot Cake

3 eggs, well beaten
2 cups sugar
1 cup vegetable oil
2 cups flour
1 teaspoon salt
2 teaspoons cinnamon
2 tablespoons baking powder
3 cups grated carrots

Preheat oven to 350 degrees. Mix eggs, sugar, and oil in a large bowl. In a separate bowl mix together the dry ingredients. Add the dry mixture into wet mixture until just mixed. Fold in carrots. Pour into greased 11" x 7" cake pan and bake at 350 degrees until center is done, about 45- 50 minutes.

Cream Cheese frosting:

½ cup (1 stick) butter
1 8- ounce package cream cheese, softened
2 cups powdered sugar
1 teaspoon vanilla
grated rind of one lemon or orange (optional)

Cream together butter and cheese. Fold in sugar. Add vanilla and zest. (Thin with a small amount of milk if necessary).

Chocolate Cake

¼ cup (1/2 stick) butter or shortening
¼ cup cocoa powder
1 cup water
¼ cup oil
2 cups sugar
2 cups flour
½ cup buttermilk
1 teaspoon baking soda
1 teaspoon vanilla
1 egg, beaten

Preheat oven to 350 degrees. Melt together butter, cocoa, water, and oil in a small saucepan and bring to a boil. Combine buttermilk and baking soda in small dish. In a separate large mixing bowl, combine sugar and flour. Add melted butter mixture to sugar and flour. Add the buttermilk and soda mixture. Add the vanilla and mix well. Fold in beaten eggs until just blended. This batter is thin. Pour into greased 11" x 7" cake pan and bake at 350 degrees for 35 minutes.

Coffee/Chocolate Chip Shortbread

I made these in preparation for an article that I wrote and took them to two different picnics. At both picnics, these got rave reviews! Everyone was guessing what was in them although I think they were using it as a guise to eat more and guess again. Kids of all ages loved these. KJG

2-½ cups butter, softened (5 sticks)
5 cups flour
¼ cup instant coffee
2 cups powdered sugar
2 tablespoons vanilla
4 cups mini-chocolate chips*

*We substituted regular- sized chips (milk chocolate is our favorite) with the thought that the more chocolate, the better.

Preheat oven to 350 degrees. Place all ingredients except the chocolate chips into a large bowl. Work together until smooth. Add chocolate chips and stir just enough to incorporate. Press dough into two greased 9" x 13" pans. Score lightly with knife into squares and perforate with fork tines so bars will cut nicely when baked and cooled.

Bake in preheated oven for 25 minutes until set and just turning golden brown. Let cool a few minutes and retrace scored lines. Cool completely in pans before cutting.

Serves a full boat (makes two pans full). These freeze well

Cranberry Applesauce Cake

1-cup butter, softened
2 cups sugar
4 eggs
1 ¾ cups applesauce
3 cups flour
1- ½ teaspoon baking soda
2-teaspoons cinnamon
1-teaspoon ground clove
½ teaspoon nutmeg
2 cups oatmeal
1 cup cranberry sauce (about ½ can)

Preheat oven to 350 degrees. Cream butter, beat in sugar and eggs. Add applesauce and blend thoroughly. Batter may look curdled. In a separate bowl, combine flour, soda and spices. Add dry mixture to applesauce mixture. Blend well. Stir in oatmeal and cranberry sauce. Pour into greased 11" x 7" cake pan and bake until middle is done, about 40 minutes. Top with maple glaze or lemon icing.

Maple Glaze
1-½ cups powdered sugar
½ cup maple syrup
Blend all ingredients to make a spreading consistency.

Lemon Icing
¼ cup lemon juice
grated rind of one lemon
1-2 cups powdered sugar
Blend all ingredients to make a spreading consistency.

Crisp – Raspberry

*You may substitute fresh berries, if you are lucky enough to
have them. You can also substitute other fruits as well. KJG*

Bottom:
1 quart (4 cups) frozen raspberries
2 cups sugar

Topping:
2 cups flour
2 teaspoons baking powder
½ teaspoon salt
2 cups sugar
2/3-cup oatmeal
¼ cup butter
2 eggs, lightly beaten

Preheat the oven to 400 degrees. Mix together the fruit and
sugar. Spread over the bottom of a lasagna pan or 9" x 13" pan.
Combine the flour, baking powder, salt, sugar and oatmeal in a
large mixing bowl. Add the butter and beaten eggs. Mix
together with fork until blended and crumbly. Spoon the
topping over the fruit evenly. Bake until top is brown, about 30
minutes.

Serve warm with whipped cream or homemade vanilla ice
cream.

Other options:
Substitute any of these ingredients for the bottom layer. Follow
the rest of the steps.

Apple: 6– 7 Granny Smith apples, peeled and sliced; 1
teaspoon cinnamon; 2 cups brown sugar.
Blueberry: 1 quart frozen or fresh blueberries (4 cups); 2 cups
sugar; ¼ cup tapioca.
Strawberry: 2 cups frozen or fresh strawberries; 2 cups fresh or
frozen rhubarb; 2 cups sugar; ¼ cup flour.

Serves 8 – 10.

Decadent Chocolate Chip Cookies

The marriage of chocolate and orange in these cookies is delightful. My sister made these and my little chocolate monster loved them. KJG

4 cups flour
1-teaspoon baking soda
1-teaspoon salt
¾ cup butter (1 ½ sticks)
¼ cup shortening or margarine
1-cup sugar
1/3-cup brown sugar
1-teaspoon vanilla
2 eggs
¼ cup maple syrup
¼ cup orange juice
6 ounces semi sweet chocolate chips (1 cup)
6 ounces vanilla chips (1 cup)
1 tablespoon freshly grated orange peel*

Preheat oven to 375 degrees. Mix the flour, baking soda and salt in a large mixing bowl. In a separate bowl, mix the butter, shortening or margarine, sugar, brown sugar, vanilla, eggs, maple syrup and orange juice. Add the flour mixture to the butter mixture. Fold in the chips and grated orange peel. Drop by rounded teaspoons on greased or parchment- covered cookie sheets.

Bake approximately ten minutes until golden brown.

*You may omit the orange peel and juice and increase the maple syrup to ½ cup total.

Makes approximately 3 dozen cookies.

Maine Crazy Pudding

This will look unlike anything else and should be a little sticky-soupy. KP

Bottom:

2/3-cup sugar
2 ½ tablespoons butter
1-¼ cups flour
1 ¼ teaspoons baking powder
1 ¼ teaspoons baking soda
¾ teaspoon salt
¾ teaspoon nutmeg
¾ cup milk
½ cup raisins

Cream together sugar and butter in a large bowl. Mix together in a separate, smaller bowl the next five dry ingredients. Alternate adding dry ingredients to the sugar/butter mixture with the milk. Fold in raisins. Spread the mixture in greased lasagna pan.

Topping:

1 ¼ cups brown sugar
2 ½ tablespoons butter
2 ½ cups boiling water
2 tablespoons plus one-teaspoon lemon juice

Preheat oven to 350 degrees. Combine all ingredients for topping and pour over bottom mixture. Bake in level oven until bottom rises to the top and becomes firm and browned, about 25 minutes. Serve warm in bowls with whipped cream.
Serves 8 – 10.

Molasses Bars - Frosted

2 ¼ cups flour
2 teaspoons baking powder
1/3-teaspoon baking soda
¾ teaspoon salt
1- ½ teaspoons cinnamon
¾ teaspoon cloves
¾ cups butter, softened
¾ cups sugar
2 eggs
¾ cups molasses
½ cup hot water

Preheat oven to 350 degrees. Combine flour, baking powder, baking soda, salt, cinnamon and cloves. In a separate, larger bowl mix the butter, sugar, eggs and molasses. Add the dry mixture to the wet mixture and blend well. Add the hot water and stir until mixed. Pour into greased brownie pan and bake at 350 degrees for 30 minutes. Frost.

Frosting:
2 tablespoons butter
1-cup confectioners sugar
1-tablespoon molasses
1-tablespoon water

Beat all ingredients together until they are smooth and it is a nice spreading consistency. Frost the cooling bars while they are still warm, but not hot. Let cool completely before slicing.

Molasses Crinkles

1 ½ cup (3 sticks) shortening or butter
2 cups brown sugar, packed
2 eggs
½ cup molasses
4 ½ cups flour
1 tablespoon plus one teaspoon baking soda
½ teaspoon salt
1-teaspoon cloves
2 teaspoons cinnamon
2-teaspoons ginger
sugar

Combine shortening, brown sugar, eggs and molasses in a large mixing bowl. In a separate, smaller bowl, mix together flour, soda, salt, cloves, cinnamon and ginger. Add the dry ingredients to the larger bowl, mixing well. Allow the cookie dough to sit overnight in refrigerator.

The next day, form dough into small balls, roll in white sugar and place on greased or parchment lined cookie sheets. Bake at 350 degrees for about 8 minutes.

Makes 6-7 dozen cookies.

Oatmeal Drop Cookies

1 cup shortening or butter (2 sticks)
2 cups sugar
½ cup brown sugar
1-cup molasses
2 ½ cups flour
2-teaspoons baking soda
2-teaspoons salt
2-teaspoons cinnamon
4 cups oatmeal
2 cups raisins

Preheat oven to 375 degrees. Combine the shortening, sugar, brown sugar and molasses in a large mixing bow. In a smaller, separate bowl, mix the flour, soda, salt, cinnamon and oatmeal. Add the dry ingredients, cup by cup to the wet ingredients, mixing well. Fold in raisins. Drop by rounded teaspoons onto greased or parchment lined cookie sheets and bake 12-15 minutes.

Makes 6-7 dozen cookies.

Peanut Butter Cookies

1 ½ cups shortening or butter (3 sticks) softened
1 ½ cups peanut butter
1 ½ cups sugar
1 ½ cups brown sugar
3 eggs
3-¾ cups flour
1 ½ teaspoons baking powder
2-¼ teaspoons baking soda
¾ teaspoon salt

In a large bowl, cream together shortening, peanut butter, both sugars and eggs. In a separate, smaller bowl, combine all dry ingredients. Pour the dry mixture into the wet mixture and blend thoroughly. Note: the batter should be chilled, best to put this together the day before you make them and let it keep cool in refrigerator. The next day, roll into 2" balls; flatten with fork dipped in flour or sugar to prevent dough from sticking to fork.

Bake at 375 degrees for 10-12 minutes for a wonderful soft cookie.

Makes 5-7 dozen.

Tangy Lemon Squares

Crust:
2/3-cup butter
½ cup powdered sugar
2 cups flour

Cut together butter and sugar, add flour to mixture and press into greased cookie sheet. Bake at 350 degrees for about 10 minutes until golden brown.

Topping:
4 eggs
2 cups sugar
1/3 cup lemon juice
2 tablespoons flour
1-teaspoon baking powder
1 tablespoon grated lemon rind

Beat together until smooth, pour onto warm crust. Bake until the finger leaves no imprint, about 20 minutes.

Toffee Squares

1-cup (1 stick) butter
1 cup packed brown sugar
1 egg yolk
1-teaspoon vanilla
2 cups flour
¼ teaspoon salt

Preheat oven to 350 degrees. Blend together butter, brown sugar, yolk, and vanilla. Add flour and salt. Press into greased brownie pan. Bake until browned and sides are pulling from edges, about 35 minutes. Top immediately.

Topping:
2 cups semi-sweet chocolate chips

Pour the chips onto bottom and return pan to oven for about one minute. Spread melted chips with knife until covering is smooth and even. On the boat, Kathy places the pans on deck or in cooler, as the chocolate won't harden in a warm galley. You may have trouble in a warm kitchen as well!

Vanilla Ice Cream

Homemade ice cream is a Friday night tradition on the Lewis R. French. We use an old-fashioned ice cream maker and everyone joins in the fun, taking turns at the crank or sitting on the maker to keep it from "walking" across the deck while it's being cranked. KP

6 eggs
2 ¼ cups plus 2 tablespoons sugar
4 cups milk
2 cups Half and Half
2 ¼ tablespoons vanilla
3 cups whipping cream

Combine eggs and sugar, beating well. Add remaining ingredients and pour mixture into the ice cream freezer can. Follow directions for your ice cream maker.

Note: If you are adding something extra, like chocolate chips or strawberries, save the additions to add just as the ice cream is starting to firm up rather than putting them into the batter at the start. Adding extras will make the hardening process take longer.

Makes 1 gallon of ice cream.

Index

Index Con.'t

Resources

- To purchase King Arthur Flour, contact:
  1-800-827-6836 or bakerscatalogue.com

- For more information about the Lewis R. French,
  including booking a cruise, contact:
  Schooner Lewis R. French
  P.O. Box 922
  Camden, ME 04843
  1-800-469-4635 or email windjam@midcoast.com

Acknowledgements

This cookbook has been years in the planning and may not have happened if one very encouraging writer, Kathleen Ganster, and one talented artist, Pat Menick, hadn't devoted a lot of time to help make this dream a reality. Thanks to all the galley crews on the Lewis R. French whose attention to their tasks taught and inspired me in so many ways, and to all the passengers on the Schooner Lewis R. French who raved over the food, asked for recipes, and offered up their own favorites for us to use. There is something special about meals prepared, served, and eaten on a windjammer vacation. It's not just the fact that it all must be done without electric gadgets on a wood-burning cook stove, sometimes under roller coaster-like conditions. It's not just the fresh air and blissfully peaceful surroundings. It's the diverse passengers who shake their heads at the sight of their empty plates and sigh happily, "I didn't think I could eat another meal after the last one, but it has all been so good!" Thanks to all of you. Without you, there would be no reason for this book. – KP

Obviously, without Kathy and Captain Dan, there would be no recipes for this book. Additionally, like any major project, there were many folks that assisted behind the scenes. I am grateful for all of them, especially: my sister, Betty Ann Alchier and my mother for helping me test the recipes; our families for eating all of the "boat dishes" – it got to the point where we would serve a dish and our kids would ask, "Is this a boat dish?"; to my very dear friend, Teri Flatley who edited the book and continuously encouraged me to write it; to my three children, Eliza, Kenton, and Cole for not only eating all of the food but for the joy they bring me everyday; and finally, to Branson, who believed in this project from day one and never let me give up the dream of publishing this book. I love you all more than I can say. - KJG

Order Form

For additional copies, please complete the following:

_____ Copies of French Cooking - $14.95 per book   _____

Shipping: $3.85 first book, $1.00 each additional book _____

Total enclosed:_____

Name: _____

Address:_____

City:_____State:_____

Zip:_____ Phone:_____

Email:_____

Please send check or money order to:

Traveling Bag Press
P.O. Box 273
Allison Park, P A 15101-0273
724-443-1664 or email <u>kganster@fyi.net</u>
Or

Schooner Lewis R. French
P.O. Box 922
Camden, ME 04843
1-800-469-4635 or email windjam@midcoast.com